D0605364

Sources for Library Materials in FY10
Albany County Public Library

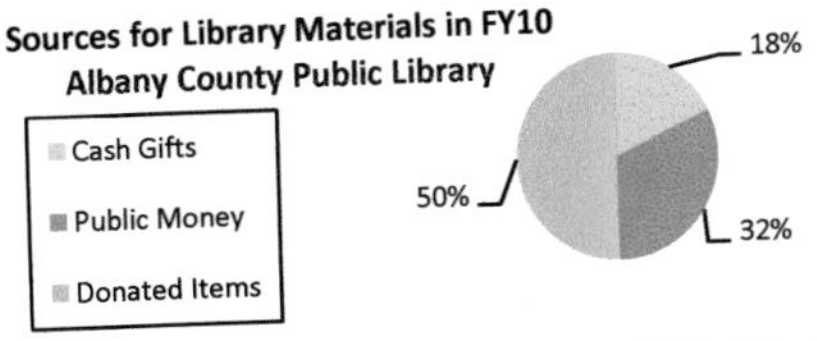

- Cash Gifts
- Public Money
- Donated Items

18%
50%
32%

Celebrate reading with us!

Cover illustration from *Fables* by Arnold Lobel. Copyright © 1980 by Arnold Lobel. Reprinted by permission of Harper & Row, Publishers, Inc., and Jonathan Cape.

Acknowledgments appear on page 233.

1995 Impression
Copyright © 1993 by Houghton Mifflin Company. All rights reserved.

Printed in the U.S.A.

ISBN: 0-395-61084-2

56789-VH-96 95 94

Silly Things Happen

Illustration from *Fables* by Arnold Lobel. Copyright © 1980 by Arnold Lobel.
Reprinted by permission of Harper & Row, Publishers, Inc. and Jonathan Cape.

Senior Author
John J. Pikulski

Senior Coordinating Author
J. David Cooper

Senior Consulting Author
William K. Durr

Coordinating Authors
Kathryn H. Au
M. Jean Greenlaw
Marjorie Y. Lipson
Susan E. Page
Sheila W. Valencia
Karen K. Wixson

Authors
Rosalinda B. Barrera
Edwina Bradley
Ruth P. Bunyan
Jacqueline L. Chaparro
Jacqueline C. Comas
Alan N. Crawford
Robert L. Hillerich
Timothy G. Johnson
Jana M. Mason
Pamela A. Mason
William E. Nagy
Joseph S. Renzulli
Alfredo Schifini

Senior Advisor
Richard C. Anderson

Advisors
Christopher J. Baker
Charles Peters
MaryEllen Vogt

HOUGHTON MIFFLIN COMPANY   BOSTON
Atlanta   Dallas   Geneva, Illinois   Palo Alto   Princeton   Toronto

3

🏅 Award Winner

6

THEME 3

138

THE WORLD OF INFORMATION

WELCOME to the BEST FRIENDS CLUB

Here you'll meet Sarunna and Ali, Ira and Reggie, and Julian and Gloria. They're already friends with each other, and now they're waiting inside to become your friends.

Club Rules:

1. Friends stay friends even if one moves away.
2. Best friends share with one another.
3. Anyone can be a best friend.

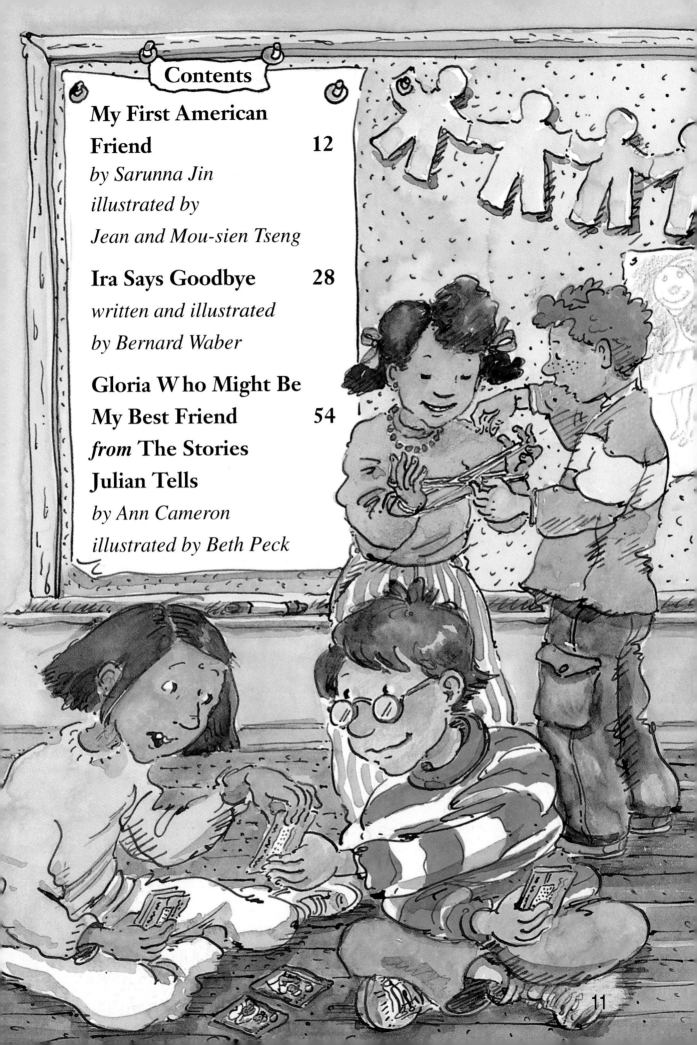

Contents

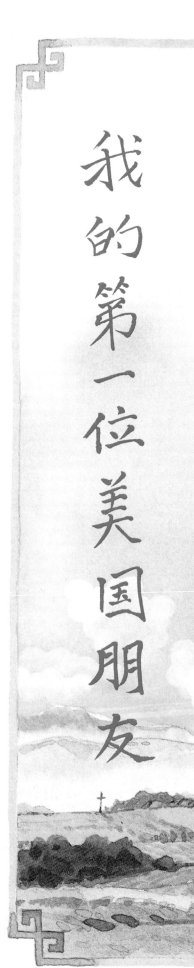

My First American Friend

我的第一位美国朋友

by *Sarunna Jin*

illustrations by Jean and Mou-sien Tseng

I was born in China. When I was two months old, I went to live with my grandparents in a place called Inner Mongolia in China. This made it possible for my parents to go to school in a different part of China. They wanted to do this so that we could all have a better life someday.

Later, my parents went to America to study at a school called Boston College. It is in the state of Massachusetts. I stayed with my grandparents in China. I was happy there with them and my friends.

When I was six years old, my parents asked me if I would like to join them in America. I said, "Okay!"

On the morning of my journey to America, I had to get up at five o'clock. My grandma and I traveled by train to Beijing, the capital of China. There we met my aunt, who took us to the airport. Even though I was so young, I was flying to America all by myself!

The trip was a real adventure. I flew from China to Japan, and from Japan to San Francisco in America. From there I flew to New York, where my mom and dad were waiting. We had a happy reunion with hugs and kisses.

Soon after I got to America, I started first grade. I didn't know any English. That made it difficult for me to do everything. I tried to talk with the other children, but we could not understand each other.

No one played with me. Oh, how sad and lonely I was for my friends that I had left behind. I felt especially sad when my mom read a letter from my grandmother. It said that one of my friends in China had knocked on my grandmother's door and asked, "Is Sarunna back yet?" That made me sadder. Then something happened to make me feel better.

I was sitting at my desk during playtime when a girl named Ali came over to play with me. Ali had blue eyes, a pretty smile, and beautiful hair. I had never seen such pretty hair before. Even though I could only speak a little bit of English, Ali and I had lots of fun together. She let me touch her pretty hair.

From that day on, we always played together at
school. Sometimes we played on the swings.
Sometimes we played on the slide.

In the classroom, we built blocks and painted together. Ali and I became best friends and were very happy!

At the end of the year, Ali told me that she was moving to another school. I was sad again because my very best friend was leaving. On the last day of school, we hugged and said good-bye.

In second grade, my English improved a lot. I still had some problems with the language, but I made many new friends.

This year, I am in the third grade, and my English is perfect! I have many friends now, and I'm very happy. But I'll always remember Ali, my first American friend.

The Language of Friendship

At first Sarunna couldn't understand her classmates, and they couldn't understand her. How would you get someone to understand you, if you couldn't use words?

Think of something to tell a partner. Help your partner to understand what you are thinking by acting it out, *not* by speaking. Then switch places. See if you can understand your partner.

Sometimes friendship speaks louder than words!

Award Winner

What Johnny Told Me

I went to play with Billy. He
Threw my cap into a tree.
I threw his glasses in the ditch.
He dipped my shirt in a bucket of pitch.
I hid his shoes in the garbage can.
And then we heard the ice cream man.
So I bought him a cone. He bought
me one.
A true good friend is a lot of fun!

John Ciardi

Two Friends

lydia and shirley have
two pierced ears and
two bare ones
five pigtails
two pairs of sneakers
two berets
two smiles
one necklace
one bracelet
lots of stripes and
one good friendship

Nikki Giovanni

Since Hanna Moved Away

The tires on my bike are flat.
The sky is grouchy gray.
At least it sure feels like that
Since Hanna moved away.

Chocolate ice cream tastes like prunes.
December's come to stay.
They've taken back the Mays and Junes
Since Hanna moved away.

Flowers smell like halibut.
Velvet feels like hay.
Every handsome dog's a mutt
Since Hanna moved away.

Nothing's fun to laugh about.
Nothing's fun to play.
They call me, but I won't come out
Since Hanna moved away.

Judith Viorst

IRA SAYS GOODBYE

written and illustrated by Bernard Waber

Reggie, my best friend, was moving away. My sister was the first to tell me about it.

This is how she told me. She said: "I . . . ra . . . !"

"What?" I said.
"Do I have a surprise for you!"
(I knew, right away, I would hate the surprise.)
"What?" I said.
"What I just heard."
(I knew, right away, I shouldn't say *what* again.)
"What?" I said again.
"Guess," she said.
"GOODBYE!" I said.

"Wait!" she said.
"Somebody is going to be doing something."
"What?" I said.
"Real soon."
"What?" I said.
"Something."
"GOODBYE!" I said.

"Wait!" she said.

"Moving," she said.

"Somebody is moving?" I said.

"In two weeks."

"Who?" I said.

"Aren't you going to guess?"

"Whooooooooooooo?" I said.

"Not even one little, teenie, tiny guess?"

"GOODBYE!" I said.

"Wait!" she said.

"Reggie!"

"What!" I said.

"Your best friend."

"Is moving?"

"Away," she said. "Far, far away.
Oh, I would hate it to pieces if my best
friend were moving away. What will you do
when your best friend in the whole wide world
moves away? Hmmmmmm?"

"I don't believe it," I said.
"Believe it," she said.

I ran into the house.

"It's true," said my mother.

"We were just coming to tell you," said my father.

"We learned about it only minutes ago," said my mother.

"But it's not as though you won't ever see Reggie again," said my father. "Greendale is only an hour's drive."

"Greendale?" I said.

"Where Reggie will be living," said my mother.

"And you can always talk on the telephone," said my father.

"But talking on the telephone won't be the same," I said.

"I know," said my mother.

"I know," said my father.

Reggie, moving! I couldn't
believe it. Reggie was my best friend
as far back as I could remember.

We had our own tree house and
a secret hiding place that only we
knew about because it was so secret.

And we had a magic act: the Amazing Reggie and the Fantastic Ira. Everyone came to see us perform.

And we had our own club: The Dolphins. So far, there were only two members — us. But we thought it was a good start.

I went to all of Reggie's birthday parties. And he came to all of mine.

We put our baseball cards together, so that way it would make a bigger pile.

When Reggie was away
on vacation, I took care
of his dog, Herman. He
did the same for
Geraldine, my cat.

And when Reggie was sick in the hospital, I sent
him a get-well card. I made it myself.

And when I was away, visiting my grandparents in
Oregon, Reggie sent me a miss-you card.

We even put our turtles together in the same tank, so they could be best friends too — like us. My turtle was Felix. His was Oscar.

I decided to go and find Reggie, and tell him how sorry I felt to hear he was moving away.

I found Reggie.
We both started talking
at the same time.
   "You're moving," I said.
   "We're moving," he said.
   "To Greendale," I said.
   "To Greendale," he said.
   And then he said, "My
father has a new job."

   "In Greendale," I said.
   Reggie sighed. I sighed too.
   "We can still talk on the telephone," I said.
   "But that won't be the same," said Reggie.
   "I know," I said.

But the next day, to my surprise, Reggie wasn't the same Reggie anymore.

"Isn't it terrible?" I said.

"Isn't it terrific?" he said.

I looked at Reggie. "Did you just say terrific?"

"Uh-huh," said Reggie.

"Did you just say uh-huh?" I said.

"Uh-huh," said Reggie.

I couldn't believe it. I said to Reggie, "When you just said uh-huh, the way you just said uh-huh, did you mean — uh-huh — you're glad you're moving?"

"Uh-huh," said Reggie.

Reggie started to explain: "Greendale is going to be so great," he said. "Great, great, great! My father told me all about it — last night. In Greendale, all people do is have fun. Fun, fun, fun, all of the time. Listen to this: There's this place in Greendale where they keep this killer shark. Every day, people go to this place to see this killer shark — just so they can get scared. Because the minute this killer shark sees everybody, he starts to snort."

"Sharks snort?" I said.

"This one snorts," said Reggie. "And he makes killer shark faces at everybody, because that's what killer sharks love best to do, make ugly, scary killer shark faces at people. Isn't that great!"

"And do you know what else about Greendale?" said
Reggie. "There's this park, with games and thriller
rides. And all people do all day, in Greendale,
is play these games, and scream their heads
off riding these thriller rides — and
watch fireworks Saturday nights.
Isn't that great!"

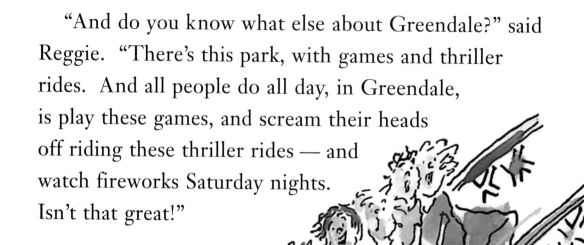

"And do you know what else about Greendale?" said Reggie. "There's this lake, with swans and ducks, and cute little baby swans and ducks too. And the minute these swans and ducks see you coming, they just scoot right up to you, just so you can feed them. Isn't that great!"

"And the people in Greendale are so friendly," said Reggie. "All they do, all day long, is go around smiling. Smiling, smiling, smiling, all of the time. They just never get tired of smiling. And they give you this big hello, no matter how many times they see you. Even if they see you two hundred times a day, they'll stop and say hello. Isn't that great!"

"People here are friendly," I said. "Some are even best friends."

But Reggie just went on talking about Greendale, as if he had never heard about best friends.

"Oh, I almost forgot the most terrific part," said Reggie, "the part about my Uncle Steve. He plays football for the Greendale Tigers, you know. And I'll be seeing him every day. And he's going to teach me to kick and pass, so that when I grow up, I'll play football for the Greendale Tigers too. Isn't that great!"

Reggie looked at me. "Isn't that great!" he said again.

"Uh-huh," I said.

Day after day, Reggie had new stories to tell about Greendale. He never seemed to want to do any of our old things anymore, like going up to the tree house or performing the magic act. He even took back his top hat, cape, and wand, which were kept at the secret hiding place. And while he was at it, he took his baseball cards. It was as if Reggie had already moved away.

One day, Reggie came by to take back Oscar, his turtle. It was my turn to keep the tank.

"But Felix and Oscar are friends," I said. "They're used to being together."

"They're only turtles," said Reggie.

"Turtles have feelings," I said. "And nobody can explain to a turtle why his friend isn't with him anymore."

"Nothing bothers turtles," said Reggie.

"Turtles are bothered. They're bothered a whole lot," I said. "Turtles get lonely. And they get sad — especially if a friend is taken away. And they start to mope."

"Turtles do not mope," said Reggie.

"They do so mope," I said. "Everybody knows that. And they stop eating. And they get sick — even die. Do you want that to happen, Reggie?"

"They don't die," said Reggie, "not from losing a friend."

"They do, too, die," I said. "Everybody knows that about turtles. Everybody who isn't stupid knows that."

"I'm taking Oscar," said Reggie.

"Then take Felix, too," I said.

Reggie looked at me. "Do you mean it?" he said.

"Uh-huh," I said.

And that's just what happened. Reggie walked out with Oscar — and Felix.

Maybe I shouldn't have said that part about being stupid. But sometimes Reggie gets to me. Sometimes Reggie really gets to me. Like whenever I call Reggie on the telephone, and I say to him, "What are you doing?" He always says, "Talking to you" — like I didn't know he was talking to me. I can't tell you how many times he pulled that one.

Do you want to know something else about Reggie? When Reggie eats lunch, he always laughs with his mouth wide open, and with all that yuckie food showing. I hate that about Reggie.

And Reggie doesn't care one bit about friends. He really doesn't. He didn't care one bit how lonely Felix and Oscar would feel without each other.

Do you want to know something? I just hope some new kid moves into Reggie's old house; some new kid who will be my best friend; some new kid who won't always be bragging about his uncle the football player.

Do you want to know something else? I can't wait for Reggie to move.

Do you want to know something else? I will jump for joy the day Reggie moves away.

I didn't have to wait long. One day, a big van pulled up to Reggie's house. I watched as the men carried everything out of the house.

When the house was empty, Reggie and his parents came outside.

Reggie was carrying the tank with Felix and Oscar in it. My parents and sister were there too. Everyone hugged and said goodbye — everyone except Reggie and me.

"Aren't you two going to say goodbye?" said Reggie's mother.

Suddenly, Reggie burst out crying and couldn't stop. He cried and cried, and no amount of patting seemed to help.

"Reggie is taking this move so hard," said his father.

At last, when Reggie stopped crying, he handed me the tank. He said, "Here, Ira, you keep them."

"You're giving Felix and Oscar to me?" I said.

"Uh-huh," said Reggie.

I was so surprised.

I dug into my pocket for my baseball cards, and handed Reggie the one I always knew he wanted.

"You're giving me your favorite card!" said Reggie.

"Uh-huh," I said.

This time it was Reggie's turn to be surprised.

We all waved goodbye as Reggie and his parents drove away. When their car disappeared, we looked at each other. Everyone was sad.

"There's only one thing to do at a time like this," said my mother.

"What?" I said.

"Let's go into the house and bake a cake."

"Excellent," said my father.

"What kind of cake?" said my sister.

"How about angel food?" said my mother.

And that's just what we did, the day Reggie moved.

We baked a cake.

That night, the telephone rang. "It's for you, Ira," said my father.

It was Reggie.
"What are you doing?" he said.
"Talking to you," I said.

"Stop fooling," said Reggie.
"I'm eating cake," I said.
"Listen," said Reggie, "would you like to visit at my house this weekend? My father and I can pick you up."
"Oh, would I!" I said. "Will your uncle Steve be there?"
"Uh-huh," said Reggie.
"Great!" I said. "I can't wait."
"Just a minute," said Reggie. "My mother wants to ask your mother if it's all right for you to come."

My mother got on the telephone.
"Say yes," I whispered.
   "Yes . . . I mean . . . hello!
Oh, hello, Ellie!"
   Ellie is Reggie's mother.
   "How are things?" said my mother.
   "Say yes," I whispered.
   My mother said, "Uh-huh."
And then she said some more "uh-huhs."
And then she said, "Yes. Yes, yes, yes,"
she kept saying.

   Yes, yes, yes, I kept shaking my head.
   And then she said, "Oh, won't that
be nice!"
   I knew what she meant by "nice."
"It will be very nice," I whispered.
   "You're sure it won't be trouble?"
she said.
   "It won't be trouble," I shook my head.
   "Saturday." My mother looked at me
hugging myself. "I know he'll be
delighted," she said.

My mother hung up. "Guess what?" she said.

"I'm invited to Reggie's house," I called out, as I ran up the stairs.

"Ira, where are you rushing to?" said my father.

"Up to pack," I said.

"But you're not leaving until Saturday," said my mother. "You have two whole days to pack."

"I don't want to be late," I said.

It Happened to Me

Even best friends can have problems. Ira had a problem because his best friend was moving away. Write a few sentences about a problem that you and one of your friends have had. Be sure to tell how you solved it.

from
**The Stories
Julian Tells**

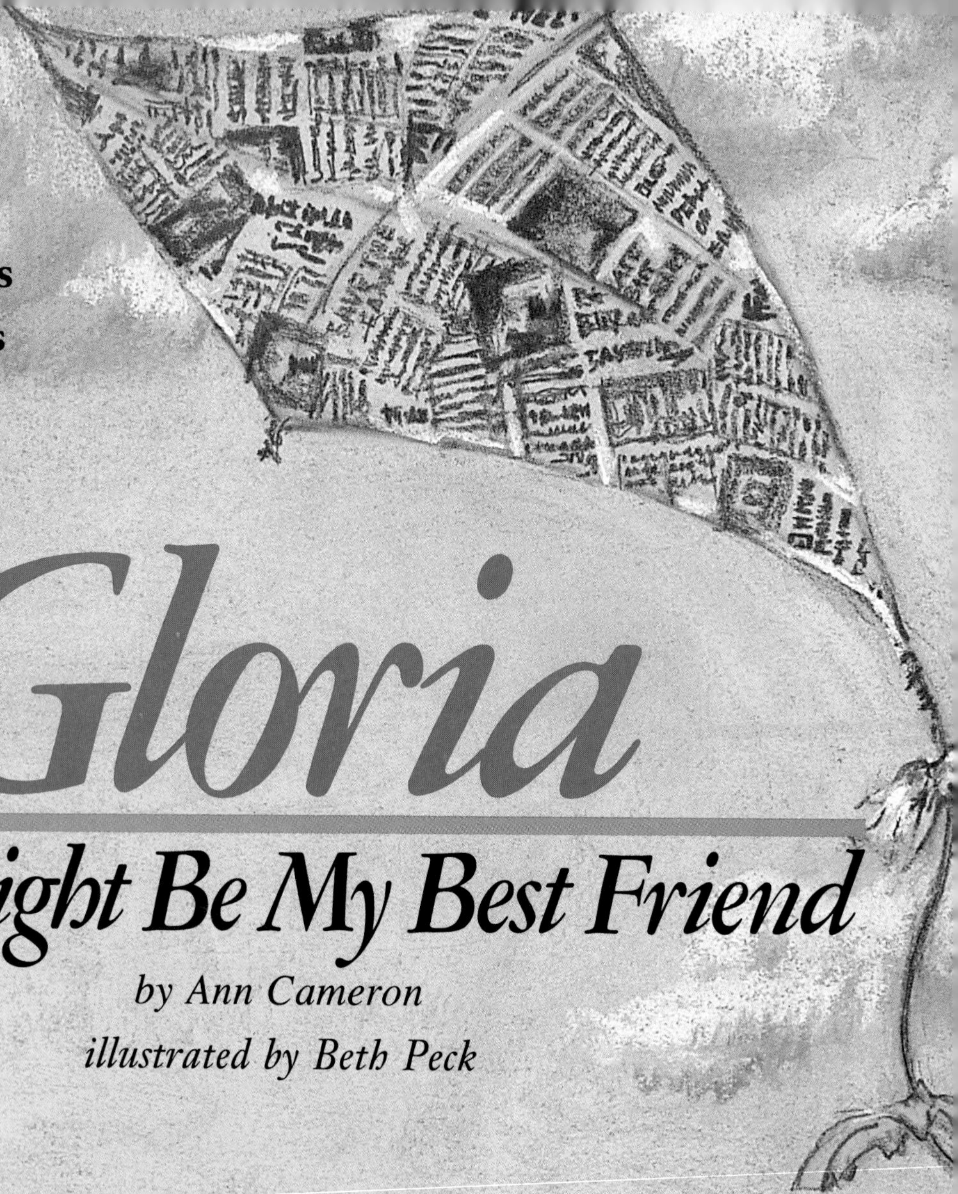

Gloria

Who Might Be My Best Friend

by Ann Cameron

illustrated by Beth Peck

If you have a girl for a friend, people find
out and tease you. That's why I didn't want a
girl for a friend — not until this summer,
when I met Gloria.

It happened one afternoon when I was walking down the street by myself. My mother was visiting a friend of hers, and Huey was visiting a friend of his. Huey's friend is five and so I think he is too young to play with. And there aren't any kids just my age. I was walking down the street feeling lonely.

A block from our house I saw a moving van in front of a brown house, and men were carrying in chairs and tables and bookcases and boxes full of I don't know what. I watched for a while, and suddenly I heard a voice right behind me.

"Who are you?"

I turned around and there was a girl in a yellow dress. She looked the same age as me. She had curly hair that was braided into two pigtails with red ribbons at the ends.

"I'm Julian," I said. "Who are you?"

"I'm Gloria," she said. "I come from Newport. Do you know where Newport is?"

I wasn't sure, but I didn't tell Gloria. "It's a town on the ocean," I said.

"Right," Gloria said. "Can you turn a cartwheel?"

She turned sideways herself and did two cartwheels on the grass.

I had never tried a cartwheel before, but I tried to copy Gloria. My hands went down in the grass, my feet went up in the air, and — I fell over.

I looked at Gloria to see if she was laughing at me. If she was laughing at me, I was going to go home and forget about her.

But she just looked at me very seriously and said, "It takes practice," and then I liked her.

"I know where there's a bird's nest in your yard," I said.

"Really?" Gloria said. "There weren't any trees in the yard, or any birds, where I lived before."

I showed her where a robin lives and has eggs. Gloria stood up on a branch and looked in. The eggs were small and pale blue. The mother robin squawked at us, and she and the father robin flew around our heads.

"They want us to go away," Gloria said. She got down from the branch, and we went around to the front of the house and watched the moving men carry two rugs and a mirror inside.

"Would you like to come over to my house?" I said.

"All right," Gloria said, "if it is all right with my mother." She ran in the house and asked.

It was all right, so Gloria and I went to my house, and I showed her my room and my games and my rock collection, and then I made strawberry punch and we sat at the kitchen table and drank it.

"You have a red mustache on your mouth," Gloria said.

"You have a red mustache on your mouth, too," I said.

Gloria giggled, and we licked off the mustaches with our tongues.

"I wish you'd live here a long time," I told Gloria.

Gloria said, "I wish I would too.

"I know the best way to make wishes," Gloria said.

"What's that?" I asked.

"First you make a kite. Do you know how to make one?"

"Yes," I said, "I know how." I know how to make good kites because my father taught me. We make them out of two crossed sticks and folded newspaper.

"All right," Gloria said, "that's the first part of making wishes that come true. So let's make a kite."

We went out into the garage and spread out sticks and newspaper and made a kite. I fastened on the kite string and went to the closet and got rags for the tail.

"Do you have some paper and two pencils?" Gloria asked. "Because now we make the wishes."

I didn't know what she was planning, but I went in the house and got pencils and paper.

"All right," Gloria said. "Every wish you want to have come true you write on a long thin piece of paper. You don't tell me your wishes, and I don't tell you mine. If you tell, your wishes don't come true. Also, if you look at the other person's wishes, your wishes don't come true."

Gloria sat down on the garage floor and started writing her wishes. I wanted to see what they were — but I went to the other side of the garage and wrote my own wishes instead. I wrote:

1. I wish I could see the catalog cats.

2. I wish the fig tree would be the tallest in town.

3. I wish I'd be a great soccer player.

4. I wish I could ride in an airplane.

5. I wish Gloria would stay here and be my best friend.

I folded my five wishes in my fist and went over to Gloria.

"How many wishes did you make?" Gloria asked.

"Five," I said. "How many did you make?"

"Two," Gloria said.

I wondered what they were.

"Now we put the wishes on the tail of the kite," Gloria said. "Every time we tie one piece of rag on the tail, we fasten a wish in the knot. You can put yours in first."

I fastened mine in, and then Gloria fastened in hers, and we carried the kite into the yard.

"You hold the tail," I told Gloria, "and I'll pull."

We ran through the back yard with the kite, passed the garden and the fig tree, and went into the open field beyond our yard.

The kite started to rise. The tail jerked heavily like a long white snake. In a minute the kite passed the roof of my house and was climbing toward the sun.

We stood in the open field, looking up at it. I was wishing I would get my wishes.

"I know it's going to work!" Gloria said.

"How do you know?"

"When we take the kite down," Gloria told me, "there shouldn't be one wish in the tail. When the wind takes all your wishes, that's when you know it's going to work."

The kite stayed up for a long time. We both held the string. The kite looked like a tiny black spot in the sun, and my neck got stiff from looking at it.

"Shall we pull it in?" I asked.

"All right," Gloria said.

We drew the string in more and more until, like a tired bird, the kite fell at our feet.

We looked at the tail. All our wishes were gone. Probably they were still flying higher and higher in the wind.

Maybe I would see the catalog cats and get to be a good soccer player and have a ride in an airplane and the tallest fig tree in town. And Gloria would be my best friend.

"Gloria," I said, "did you wish we would be friends?"

"You're not supposed to ask me that!" Gloria said.

"I'm sorry," I answered. But inside I was smiling. I guessed one thing Gloria wished for. I was pretty sure we would be friends.

DON'T TELL YOUR WISHES,
WHATEVER YOU DO.
THEN MAYBE YOUR WISHES
WILL ALL COME TRUE!

MY WISH KITE

Make a wish kite
with one of your friends.
Here are the things
you will need:

- a large piece of colored paper
- six small pieces of paper
- tape, scissors
- a long piece of string
- a pencil and crayons

First draw a kite on the large piece of paper. Then cut out the kite. Next, tape a piece of string on for the tail. Then you and your friend should each write three wishes on the small pieces of paper. Finally, tape your wishes onto the tail of the kite.

About the Authors and Illustrators

Sarunna Jin was eight years old when she wrote *My First American Friend.* She still visits her friend Ali, who lives in a nearby town. Sarunna has also written poems, reports, and adventure stories. She likes reading mystery books, and her favorite author is Beverly Cleary.

Sarunna's advice to people who have trouble writing is to start by taking notes about the things they like. Sarunna enjoys swimming, skating, gymnastics, playing the piano, and riding her bicycle.

Jean and Mou-sien Tseng were born in Taiwan. They met when they were art students and have worked together ever since. In one of their biggest projects, they designed 165 children's books for UNICEF and illustrated 30 of them! One of their award-winning picture books is *Seven Chinese Brothers*.

The Tsengs now live on Long Island, New York. They love to travel and have recently returned from a journey through Inner Mongolia, China.

More Authors and Illustrators

Bernard Waber began writing and illustrating children's books when his own children were growing up. After Bernard Waber wrote stories about Lyle the Crocodile, his friends gave him presents shaped like crocodiles. Soon his house was full of all kinds of crocodiles!

You may enjoy reading other books by Bernard Waber. In *Ira Sleeps Over*, Reggie invites Ira to spend the night. This story takes place before *Ira Says Goodbye*.

A CROCODILE and BIRD

BY José

by Lisa

"HELP!"

Ann Cameron had a friend named Julian who told her many funny stories about his childhood. Her friend's funny stories gave Ann Cameron the idea of writing a book about growing up.

You might like to read more about Julian in the books *More Stories Julian Tells* and *Julian's Glorious Summer.*

Beth Peck is the illustrator of *Matthew and Tilly,* another book about two best friends. She has also illustrated many other books for children, including *The Silver Whistle, Time of the Bison,* and *Sarah and the Dragon.*

More Clubhouse Reading

Henry and Mudge
by Cynthia Rylant
Henry and his dog Mudge are the best of friends and do everything together.

Everett Anderson's Friend
by Lucille Clifton
When Maria moves next door, Everett finds that girls make good friends.

Earl's Too Cool for Me
by Leah Komaiko
A boy thinks that Earl can do anything. Would Earl ever want to be his friend?

Matthew and Tilly

by Rebecca C. Jones

Matthew and Tilly are friends —
until they get sick of each other.
Will they ever play together again?

Nice New Neighbors

by Franz Brandenberg

Everybody seems too busy to make
friends with the new children
in the neighborhood.

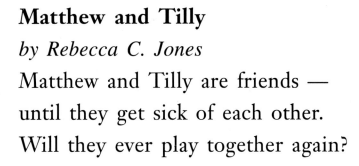

73

Award Winner

Meet
Jeff Moss

For many years Jeff Moss was the head writer for the television program *Sesame Street*. It was Jeff Moss who created the character of Cookie Monster. He has written many songs for the program, too, including the song "Rubber Duckie."

Jeff Moss is also a writer of poetry for children. His book, *The Butterfly Jar*, contains over eighty poems about everything from washing your neck to eating ice cream to the things monsters are most afraid of.

IN BETWEEN

My sister goes out to the movies
My brother stays home in his crib.
I'm too young to go with my sister
And too old for wearing a bib.
Too grown-up to be baby-sat for,
But too young to go baby-sit.
So if there's one age that is lousy,
I'll tell you for sure, this is it.

MOVING

Mom and Dad told us we're moving
To a better city
With a nicer house
And a better school
With great new friends
And even the weather will be sunnier.

What I want to know is
If everything's so great where we're moving
How come we didn't decide to live there in the first place?

75

IF I FIND A PENNY

If I find a penny
And give it to you,
That means we'll both
Have a wish come true.
A penny is like magic
Lying on the ground.
It's like picking up a wish
That's waiting to be found.

So when I find one,
I'll give you a penny.
And if we're lucky
I'll give you many.
I'll pick up your penny,
Won't let the trashman sweep it.
But if I find a dollar . . .
I'll probably keep it.

COW IN THE CITY

A cow took a trip to the city one day.

She nibbled on the sidewalk 'cause there wasn't any hay.

She mooed at the cars 'cause there weren't any sheep.

And at night she went to a hotel to sleep.

She got into bed and it broke with a crash,

So back to the country she ran in a flash,

And safe in her barn, mooed a long happy moo.

(If I were a cow, that's what I'd do, too.)

IT'S DARK OUT HERE!
WHY DID AMELIA BEDELIA PUT THE LIGHT BULBS OUTSIDE?
OPEN THE DOOR!
WHY DID THE WOLF MAKE ONE HUNDRED PANCAKES?
SYRUP
WHAT IS PART HEN, PART DUCK, PART COW, PART CAT AND PART DOG?

TO FIND OUT THE ANSWERS TO THESE THREE RIDDLES, READ *FUNNY BUSINESS!*

SALT

TABLE OF CONTENTS

The Wolf's Chicken Stew

Keiko Kasza

There once lived a wolf who loved to eat more than anything else in the world. As soon as he finished one meal, he began to think of the next.

One day the wolf got
a terrible craving for
chicken stew.

All day long he
walked across the forest in
search of a delicious chicken.
Finally he spotted one.

"Ah, she is just perfect for my
stew," he thought.

The wolf crept closer. But
just as he was about to grab his
prey . . . he had another idea.

"If there were just some way to
fatten this bird a little more," he
thought, "there would be all the
more stew for me."

So . . . the wolf ran
home to his kitchen, and
he began to cook.

SUGAR-SU

FLOUR

PANCAKE

First he made a hundred scrumptious pancakes. Then, late at night, he left them on the chicken's porch.

"Eat well, my pretty chicken," he cried. "Get nice and fat for my stew!"

The next night he brought a hundred scrumptious doughnuts.

"Eat well, my pretty chicken," he cried. "Get nice and fat for my stew!"

And on the next night he brought a scrumptious cake weighing a hundred pounds.

"Eat well, my pretty chicken," he cried. "Get nice and fat for my stew!"

At last, all was ready.
This was the night he had
been waiting for. He put
a large stew pot on the
fire and set out joyfully to
find his dinner.

"That chicken must be as fat as a balloon by now," he thought. "Let's see."

But as he peeked into the chicken's house . . . the door opened suddenly and the chicken screeched, "Oh, so it was you, Mr. Wolf!"

"Children, children! Look, the pancakes and the doughnuts and that scrumptious cake — they weren't from Santa Claus! All those presents were from Uncle Wolf!"

The baby chicks jumped all over the wolf and gave him a hundred kisses.

"Oh, thank you, Uncle Wolf! You're the best cook in the world!"

Uncle Wolf didn't have chicken stew that night but Mrs. Chicken fixed him a nice dinner anyway.

"Aw, shucks," he thought, as he walked home, "maybe tomorrow I'll bake the little critters a hundred scrumptious cookies!"

"OH, THANK YOU, UNCLE WOLF!"

Uncle Wolf says that he may bake a hundred scrumptious cookies for the baby chicks. If he does, the chicks will certainly want to thank him. Write a thank-you song for the chicks to sing to Uncle Wolf. Use a tune you already know, like "Twinkle, Twinkle, Little Star," "Happy Birthday," or "Who's Afraid of the Big Bad Wolf?" Then, if you want, sing your song to your classmates.

The Portrait

by Ivar Da Coll

"What a lovely morning!" said Eusebio the tiger. "So fresh, so clean! It's a perfect day for drawing."

Eusebio taped a sheet of paper to a board. Then he gathered together his pencils, eraser, and pencil sharpener, and started on his way.

"Yes, indeed," Eusebio said to himself. "It's a very good day to be me!"

At the edge of the woods, Eusebio found a spot by a tree. He sat down, smoothed his whiskers, and was about to draw his first lines when along came Úrsula the hen.

"What are you doing?" asked Úrsula.

"I am getting ready to draw."

"And how good are you at drawing?"

"I'm like a master," said Eusebio modestly.

"Well, then, make a portrait of me," said Úrsula. "I feel beautiful today. Notice my comb, my beak, my eyes . . ."

"Please don't move."

"I will be as still as a stone until the end," Úrsula promised.

She sat down quietly next to the tree. Eusebio gave all his attention to drawing her.

Suddenly Úrsula jumped up. "I left an egg cooking on the stove!" she squawked. "I must fly home or it will burn! Good-by!"

Eusebio was about to erase the lines he had drawn when along came Ananías the duck.

"How well you draw," said Ananías.

"Just like a master," agreed Eusebio, modestly scratching his ear.

"Well, draw a portrait of me," said Ananías. "I just bathed in the pool and I feel adorable. Notice my neck and my right foot. Aren't they charming?"

"Very charming, dear Ananías. Please don't move."

"I will be as still as a statue until the end," Ananías promised. Eusebio began to draw.

Suddenly Ananías jumped up. "I left the faucet on in the sink!" he quacked. "The house will be flooded! I know how to swim, but the furniture doesn't! What will I do if my furniture drowns?" Ananías said good-by and flew off.

Eusebio was about to erase the lines he had drawn. Along came Eulalia the cow, looking elegant and smelling sweet.

"What are you making?" asked Eulalia.

"A masterpiece," said Eusebio. Modestly he scratched his other ear.

"I'll help you," said Eulalia. "Draw my portrait. I look wonderful today. With a model such as I, you are sure to make a masterpiece. Notice my horns, my ears, and my tail."

"Your wish is my command, my dear Eulalia," said Eusebio. "Please don't move."

"I won't breathe a sigh until the end," promised Eulalia. Eusebio began to draw.

Suddenly Eulalia jumped up, looking worried. "Did I leave it open or closed?" she mooed.

"Did you leave what?"

"The door!" said Eulalia. "I don't remember if I closed it well when I went out. And what about the windows? The wind could blow in and make a mess of the letter I'm writing to Camila! I'm only on page five! No, we will have to continue on another day!"

Just as Eulalia was saying good-by, along came Camila the cat. "Camila! I will be sending you a ten page letter," Eulalia told her. "Please write back immediately after you get it."

Meanwhile Eusebio was saying to himself, "I think I'd better draw something else. Flowers, trees, clouds . . . anything but portraits."

"You make portraits?" said Camila. "Draw one of me! I just washed my whiskers. See? Don't you think they're beautiful?"

"Very nice. Please don't move!"

"I won't even blink," Camila promised. She lay down by a rock.

The morning sun felt so warm on her fur that her eyes slowly closed until she was fast asleep. She dreamed of the letter Eulalia was sending her. In the letter, Eulalia invited her over to eat caramels. She licked her lips.

"Camila!" said Eusebio. "Wake up! I can't draw you like that!"

But Camila was too busy dreaming about caramels to answer.

"Things don't always work out the way you want them to," sighed Eusebio. "I'm going to erase all of this and start over. I'll try to draw some flowers, trees, clouds . . ."

"One minute," said Horatio the dog, who had just arrived. "Let me see."

"It's just a masterpiece," said Eusebio modestly, scratching his ears.

"Oh, this is funny!" Horatio howled. "It's really very funny!" He fell down laughing.

"You know what? You're right," said Eusebio. "I hadn't noticed."

Horatio's laughter woke up Camila, who came over to see what was so funny. Then along came Úrsula, who had fixed her breakfast egg, and Ananías, who had turned off the faucet, and Eulalia, who had made sure the doors and windows were closed. They all fell down laughing.

"My comb is lovely," cackled Úrsula.

"Not as lovely as my foot," quacked Ananías.

"My horns are the best part," mooed Eulalia.

"And how about my tail?" mewed Camila.

"This is my best portrait," said Eusebio, chuckling.

"A masterpiece!" they all agreed.

"I must admit," said Eusebio. "It *is* a very good day to be me." And he modestly scratched both of his ears.

A FUNNY MASTERPIECE

Be an artist like Eusebio. Draw a funny portrait of a friend. Get together all the art supplies you need. Then have your friend sit still while you draw. After you're through with the portrait, you may want to give it a title. Now switch places and let your friend draw you!

Poems
to Make
You Laugh

My Fat Cat

My fat cat

snoozing in the hay

zz zz zz zz

dreaming of the little mouse

the chummy mouse

the yummy mouse

the kind that fills-your-tummy mouse

who

      got

            away.

Gato mío, gato gordo

snoozing in the hay

zz zz zz zz

dreaming of the little mouse

ratoncito pequeñito

amiguito

sabrosito

zz zz zz zz

who

      got

            away.

Charlotte Pomerantz

The Folk Who Live in Backward Town

The folk who live in Backward Town

Are inside out and upside down.

They wear their hats inside their heads

And go to sleep beneath their beds.

They only eat the apple peeling

And take their walks across the ceiling.

Mary Ann Hoberman

A Puppy

A puppy whose hair was so flowing
There really was no means of knowing
    Which end was his head,
    Once stopped me and said,
"Please, sir, am I coming or going?"

Oliver Herford

Eletelephony

Once there was an elephant,
Who tried to use the telephant—
No! No! I mean an elephone
Who tried to use the telephone—
(Dear me I am not certain quite
That even now I've got it right.)

Howe'er it was he got his trunk
Entangled in the telephunk;
The more he tried to get it free,
The louder buzzed the telephee—
(I fear I'd better drop the song
Of elephop and telephong!)

Laura E. Richards

Banananananananana

I thought I'd win the spelling bee
    And get right to the top,
But I started to spell "banana,"
    And I didn't know when to stop.

William Cole

At the Beach

—Johnny, Johnny, let go of that crab!
    You have only ten fingers, you know:
    If you hold it that way, it is certain to grab
    At least one or two of them. Please, let go!

—Thank you, Daddy, for teaching not scolding,
    But there's one thing I think you should know:
    I believe it's the crab that is doing the holding—
    I let go—OUCH!—ten minutes ago!

John Ciardi

There Was a Sad Pig with a Tail

There was a sad pig with a tail

Not curly, but straight as a nail.

So he ate simply oodles

Of pretzels and noodles,

Which put a fine twist to his tail.

Arnold Lobel

Once in the Streets of Caracas

Once in the streets of Caracas

There appeared twenty-five vacas.

Since it was Carnival,

No one there cared at all

That they danced while playing maracas.

Maria Elena Walsh

Amelia Bedelia

by Peggy Parish
Pictures by Fritz Siebel

"Oh, Amelia Bedelia, your first day of work. And I can't be here. But I made a list for you. You do just what the list says," said Mrs. Rogers. Mrs. Rogers got into the car with Mr. Rogers. They drove away.

"My, what nice folks. I'm going to like working here," said Amelia Bedelia.

Amelia Bedelia went inside. "Such a grand house. These must be rich folks. But I must get to work. Here I stand just looking. And me with a whole list of things to do."

Amelia Bedelia stood there a minute longer. "I think I'll make a surprise for them. I'll make a lemon-meringue pie. I do make good pies."

So Amelia Bedelia went into the kitchen. She put a little of this and a pinch of that into a bowl. She mixed and she rolled. Soon her pie was ready to go into the oven.

"There," said Amelia Bedelia. "That's done. Now let's see what this list says."

Amelia Bedelia read,

Change the towels in the green bathroom.

Amelia Bedelia found the green bathroom.

"Those towels are very nice. Why change them?" she thought. Then Amelia Bedelia remembered what Mrs. Rogers had said. She must do just what the list told her.

"Well, all right," said Amelia Bedelia.

Amelia Bedelia got some scissors. She snipped a little here and a little there. And she changed those towels.

"There," said Amelia Bedelia. She looked at her list again.

Dust the furniture.

"Did you ever hear tell of such a silly thing? At my house we undust the furniture. But to each his own way."

Amelia Bedelia took one last look at the bathroom. She saw a big box with the words *Dusting Powder* on it.

"Well, look at that. A special powder to dust with!" exclaimed Amelia Bedelia.

So Amelia Bedelia dusted the furniture.

"That should be dusty enough. My, how nice it smells."

Draw the drapes when the sun comes in.

read Amelia Bedelia. She looked up. The sun was
coming in. Amelia Bedelia looked at the list again.

"Draw the drapes? That's what it says. I'm not
much of a hand at drawing, but I'll try."

So Amelia Bedelia sat right down and she drew
those drapes. Amelia Bedelia marked off about
the drapes.

"Now what?"

Put the lights out when you finish in the living room.

Amelia Bedelia thought about this a minute. She switched off the lights. Then she carefully unscrewed each bulb. And Amelia Bedelia put the lights out.

"So those things need to be aired out, too. Just like pillows and babies. Oh, I do have a lot to learn."

"My pie!" exclaimed Amelia Bedelia. She hurried to the kitchen.

"Just right," she said. She took the pie out of the oven and put it on the table to cool. Then she looked at the list.

Measure two cups of rice.

"That's next," said Amelia Bedelia. Amelia Bedelia found two cups. She filled them with rice. And Amelia Bedelia measured that rice.

Amelia Bedelia laughed. "These folks do want me to do funny things." Then she poured the rice back into the container.

The meat market will deliver a steak and a chicken.

Please trim the fat before you put the steak in the icebox.

And please dress the chicken.

When the meat arrived, Amelia Bedelia opened the bag. She looked at the steak for a long time.

"Yes," she said. "That will do nicely."

Amelia Bedelia got some lace and bits of ribbon. And Amelia Bedelia trimmed that fat before she put the steak in the icebox.

"Now I must dress the chicken. I wonder if she wants a he chicken or a she chicken?" said Amelia Bedelia.

Amelia Bedelia went right to work. Soon the chicken was finished.

Amelia Bedelia heard the door open.

"The folks are back," she said. She rushed out to meet them.

"Amelia Bedelia, why are all the light bulbs outside?" asked Mr. Rogers.

"The list just said to put the lights out," said Amelia Bedelia. "It didn't say to bring them back in. Oh, I do hope they didn't get aired too long."

"Amelia Bedelia, the sun will fade the furniture. I asked you to draw the drapes," said Mrs. Rogers.

"I did! I did! See," said Amelia Bedelia. She held up her picture.

Then Mrs. Rogers saw the furniture. "The furniture!" she cried.

"Did I dust it well enough?" asked Amelia Bedelia. "That's such nice dusting powder."

Mr. Rogers went to wash his hands. "I say," he called. "These are very unusual towels."

Mrs. Rogers dashed into the bathroom. "Oh, my best towels," she said.

"Didn't I change them enough?" asked Amelia Bedelia.

Mrs. Rogers went to the kitchen. "I'll cook the dinner. Where is the rice I asked you to measure?"

"I put it back in the container. But I remember — it measured four and a half inches," said Amelia Bedelia.

"Was the meat delivered?" asked Mrs. Rogers.

"Yes," said Amelia Bedelia. "I trimmed the fat just like you said. It does look nice."

Mrs. Rogers rushed to the icebox. She opened it.

"Lace! Ribbons! Oh, dear!" said Mrs. Rogers.

"The chicken — you dressed the chicken?" asked Mrs. Rogers.

"Yes, and I found the nicest box to put him in," said Amelia Bedelia.

"Box!" exclaimed Mrs. Rogers.

Mrs. Rogers hurried over to the box. She lifted the lid. There lay the chicken. And he was just as dressed as he could be.

Mrs. Rogers was angry. She was very angry. She opened her mouth. Mrs. Rogers meant to tell Amelia Bedelia she was fired. But before she could get the words out, Mr. Rogers put something in her mouth. It was so good Mrs. Rogers forgot about being angry.

"Lemon-meringue pie!" she exclaimed.

"I made it to surprise you," said Amelia Bedelia happily. So right then and there Mr. and Mrs. Rogers decided that Amelia Bedelia must stay. And so she did.

Mrs. Rogers learned to say undust the furniture, unlight the lights, close the drapes, and things like that. Mr. Rogers didn't care if Amelia Bedelia trimmed all of his steaks with lace.

All he cared about was having her there to make lemon-meringue pie.

DON'T FORGET TO...

In the story, Mrs. Rogers left a list of jobs for Amelia to do, and Amelia got everything mixed up. Imagine that Mrs. Rogers left the list at the top of this page for Amelia.

With a partner, act out each job on the list. Take turns acting out the way Mrs. Rogers wants the job done and the way Amelia Bedelia might really do the job.

About the Authors and Illustrators

Keiko Kasza

Keiko Kasza started writing books in Japan, where she was born. While living there, she wrote and illustrated several children's books in Japanese. Kasza now lives in the United States. *The Wolf's Chicken Stew* is the first book she has published here.

Ivar Da Coll

Ivar Da Coll lives in Bogotá, Colombia, with his two cats, Sara and Eusebio. He enjoys inventing animal characters, drawing them, and then writing stories about them. Eusebio and his friends appear in other stories Ivar Da Coll has written. You may have read one of them, "The Birthday Cake," in *Bookworm*. These animal characters have also appeared on television and in the theater.

Peggy Parish

When Peggy Parish was a child, she enjoyed playing with other children. But she also enjoyed being alone because she could read as many books as she wanted. She loved books so much that when she grew up she wrote her own books. *Amelia Bedelia* was her first book about Amelia the maid. At the library, you'll find other books about Amelia Bedelia's mixed-up adventures.

Fritz Siebel

Fritz Siebel was born in Austria. After moving to the United States, he worked as an illustrator of advertisements for magazines and television. He has illustrated two other Amelia Bedelia books, as well as *Cat and Dog, Tell Me Some More,* and *Who Took the Farmer's Hat?*

A Laugh From Cover To Cover

Monkey-Monkey's Trick
by Patricia McKissack

Monkey-Monkey needs to build a new home. A pot of stew and a beautiful creature may be able to help him.

Swamp Monsters
by Mary Blount Christian

Anything can happen when two naughty swamp monsters dress up as children and go on a class trip.

The Stupids Step Out
by Harry Allard

Here are the Stupids —
a family who walk on their
hands and eat mashed potato
sundaes!

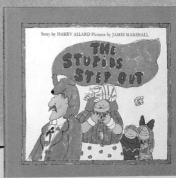

Henry Goes West
by Robert Quackenbush

Lots of silly things happen
when Henry goes out West
to visit his friend Clara.

WATER HOLE

THE
WORLD
OF
INFORMATION

- What is bigger than a million earths all put together?
- What is a stegosaurus (steg-uh-SAW-russ)?
- Who was Martin Luther King, Jr.?

Nonfiction books tell about real people, real animals, and real places. They answer questions, explain how things work, and tell about things that actually happened.

You will find the answers to the questions on page 139 in the nonfiction selections in this book. For other questions you might have, your library is full of nonfiction books on every subject you can imagine.

Welcome to the World of Information.

CONTENTS

Do You Know About Stars?

by Mae Blacker Freeman

illustrated by Fred Lynch

Look up at the sky at night. You can see many stars. They shine and twinkle.

There are

millions

of millions

of millions

of millions

of stars in the sky. There are so many stars in the sky — more than you could ever count.

When you look at a star, it seems so tiny. All things look tiny when they are far away from you. Even big things look tiny if they are far away.

An airplane is very big. It can hold many people. But . . . look at an airplane when it is high in the sky. Then it does not look big at all. It looks like a toy. The airplane looks tiny because it is far away.

Stars look tiny, too, because they are far away. But stars are really big, big, big. Some stars are much bigger than the whole earth.

All stars are far, far away. But there is one star that is not as far away as the others.

It is a star that you know very well because you see it shine in the daytime. Do you know which star it is?

It is the sun. . . . The sun is a star! The sun is big and round and very, very bright. The sun does not look tiny like the other stars. That is because the other stars are much farther away than the sun. The sun is bigger than a million earths all put together.

Can you ride
an airplane to a
star? No. There is no
air out in space. A plane
can fly only where there is air.
But a rocket can go to the sun.
It takes many months to get there. A
rocket could even go on, to the next star.
But nobody could ride in that rocket. The
trip would take too long. The trip would take
thousands of years.

Suppose you could get near the sun or near any other star. What would it look like? The sun would look like a huge ball of clouds. But the clouds are not like the fluffy white ones that you see in a blue sky. And they are not like the dark gray clouds that you see on a rainy day.

A star is made of clouds that are different. They are very, very bright and very, very hot. The clouds of a star are orange and yellow and white. They tumble and toss and swoop and swirl. Huge red flares shoot out and loop back again.

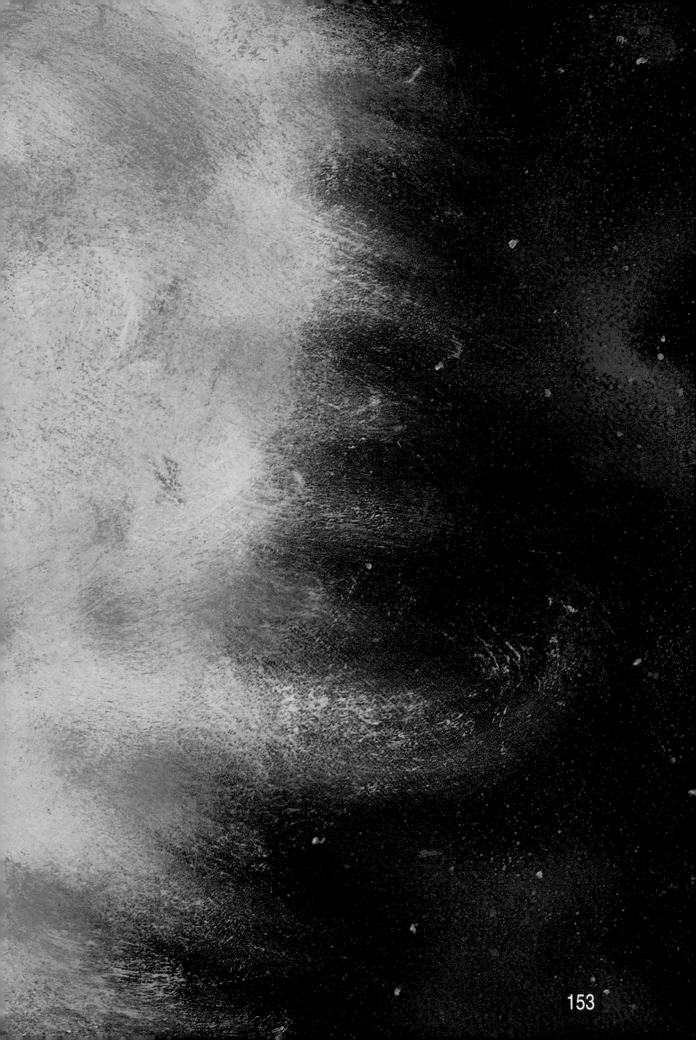

Even if you could
get near the sun or any
other star, you could not look
at it. It is much too bright. You must
never look right at the sun, even from here
on earth. It would harm your eyes.
How hot is a star? Think of some things
that are hot. Think of a hot summer day . . .
or hot sand on the beach. Think of

FIRE!

Are any of these things
as hot as a star?

No! A star is much, much hotter. A star is hotter than anything you can think of.

But YOU cannot feel how hot a star is. YOU cannot tell that a star is a ball of hot clouds that tumble and toss and swoop and swirl. The stars are too far away.

For YOU, stars are bright dots that twinkle in the dark sky. Look up at the sky tonight and see.

Now I Know About Stars

On a sheet of paper, draw a large star. On each of the five points of the star, write a fact that you have learned about the stars. Follow the steps below to help you draw your star.

How to draw a star in five easy steps

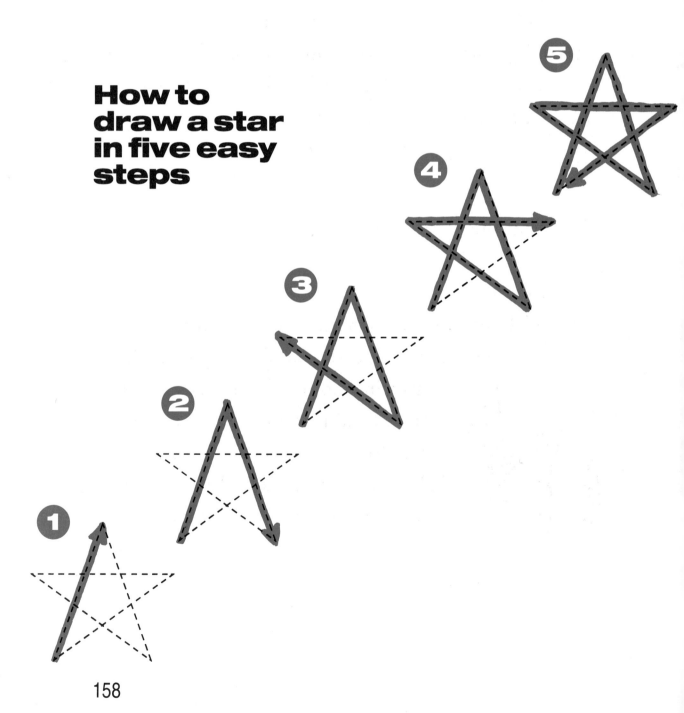

About the Author

Mae Blacker Freeman

Mae Blacker Freeman writes informational books on many different subjects. She is a photographer as well as a writer. One book that she wrote about ballet included pictures of her daughter as the ballet dancer.

Another book by Mae Blacker Freeman that is full of interesting facts is *Do You Know About Water?*

About the Illustrator

Fred Lynch

Fred Lynch always wanted to be an artist. He spent a lot of time drawing when he was growing up in Rhode Island. Now he teaches illustration at two colleges there. Fred Lynch has illustrated books, magazines, and advertisements, and has won several awards for his work.

Stars in the Sea

Did you know that there are animals shaped like stars? They are called sea stars, or **starfish.**

Starfish live in the ocean. You can often find them just by walking on the beach. They grow in many sizes, shapes, and colors.

Most starfish have five arms. Some have even more! If a starfish breaks off an arm, it can grow a new one. This makes starfish very different from most animals.

Dinosaur Time

by Peggy Parish

with illustrations by Arnold Lobel

Long, long ago the world was different.
More of the world was warm. And dinosaurs
lived in the world. . . .

There were big dinosaurs. There were
small ones. There were fast dinosaurs, and
slow ones. Some dinosaurs ate meat. Some
ate plants.

Stegosaurus

STEGOSAURUS

This is how you say it —
steg-uh-SAW-russ

This dinosaur had plates on its back.
They were made of bone. It had sharp points
on its tail. It ate plants. Its name is
Stegosaurus.

ANKYLOSAURUS

This is how you say it —
ank-eye-loh-SAW-russ

This dinosaur had a shell like a turtle. Its
tail was like a club. Not many animals could
hurt it. Its name is Ankylosaurus.

COMPSOGNATHUS

This is how you say it —
comp-soh-NAYTH-uss

This dinosaur was small. It was as big as
a cat. But it could run fast. It could catch
other animals and eat them. Its name is
Compsognathus.

Ankylosaurus

Compsognathus

BRONTOSAURUS

This is how you say it —

bron-tuh-SAW-russ

This dinosaur was a giant. But its mouth was tiny. It ate plants. It ate, and ate, and ate to fill up its big body. Its name is Brontosaurus.

PENTACERATOPS

This is how you say it —
pen-tuh-SARE-ah-tops

This dinosaur had five horns. They were
all on its face. Its name is Pentaceratops.
This name is just right. It means
"five-horns-on-the-face."

DIPLODOCUS

This is how you say it —
dip-LAH-duh-cuss

This dinosaur was long. But most of it was neck and tail. Its teeth were short and dull. It ate plants. Its name is Diplodocus.

Teratosaurus

TERATOSAURUS

This is how you say it —
tare-at-oh-SAW-russ

This dinosaur walked on its back legs. It had big claws, and sharp teeth. It ate meat. Its name is Teratosaurus.

ANATOSAURUS

This is how you say it —
an-at-oh-SAW-russ

This dinosaur is called a "duckbill." It had a beak like a duck. Its beak had no teeth. But its mouth did. There were hundreds of teeth in it! Sometimes a tooth broke. But that did not matter. It could grow a new one. Its name is Anatosaurus.

ORNITHOMIMUS

This is how you say it —
or-nith-oh-MY-muss

This dinosaur had a beak, too. But it had no teeth. It ate small animals and insects. Maybe it ate fruits and dinosaur eggs, too. But it had no teeth. How did it eat? A bird eats. It has no teeth. Maybe it ate like a bird. Its name is Ornithomimus.

Anatosaurus

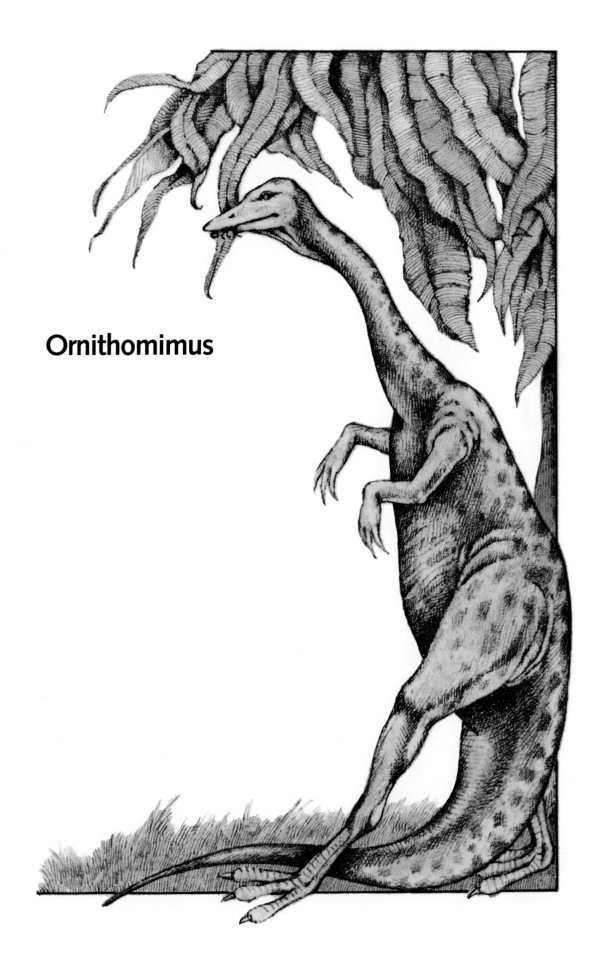

Ornithomimus

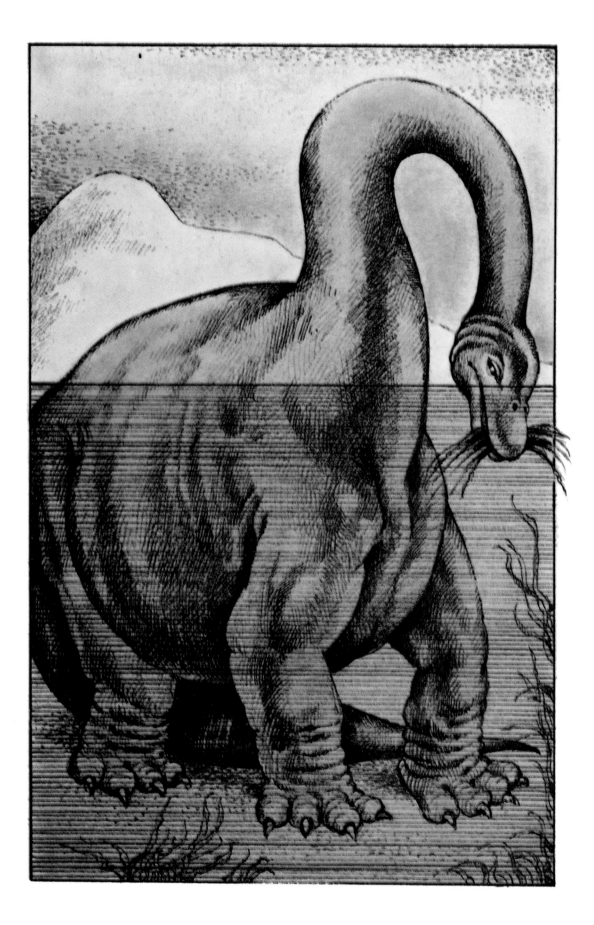

BRACHIOSAURUS

This is how you say it —
brack-ee-oh-SAW-russ

This dinosaur was fat. It was too fat to run from enemies. It ate plants. Its name is Brachiosaurus.

TYRANNOSAURUS

This is how you say it —
tih-ran-uh-SAW-russ

This dinosaur was the biggest meat-eater.
Its jaws were huge. Its teeth were six inches
long. It ate other dinosaurs. Its name is
Tyrannosaurus.

Dinosaurs lived for a long time. Then
they died. Nobody knows why. But once it
was their world. It was dinosaur time.

DINOSAUR FACTS

In this story you learned about different kinds of dinosaurs. Which kind of dinosaur did you think was the most interesting? Discuss with a partner the dinosaur you liked best. Then tell your partner some facts about that dinosaur.

About the Author
Peggy Parish

Peggy Parish was a third grade teacher before she began writing books for children. You may have already read *Amelia Bedelia,* one of her funniest books.

Another nonfiction book by this author is *Beginning Mobiles.* In this book you can learn how to make easy holiday decorations.

About the Illustrator
Arnold Lobel

Arnold Lobel illustrated almost one hundred children's books. Some of these, such as *Dinosaur Time,* were written by others. Some were written by Arnold Lobel himself. Many of his books are award winners.

Arnold Lobel especially loved illustrating science books. He said, "When you do a science book, you become a kind of mini-expert on what you're doing." He also loved a challenge. For *Dinosaur Time* the challenge was getting giant dinosaurs into a very small book!

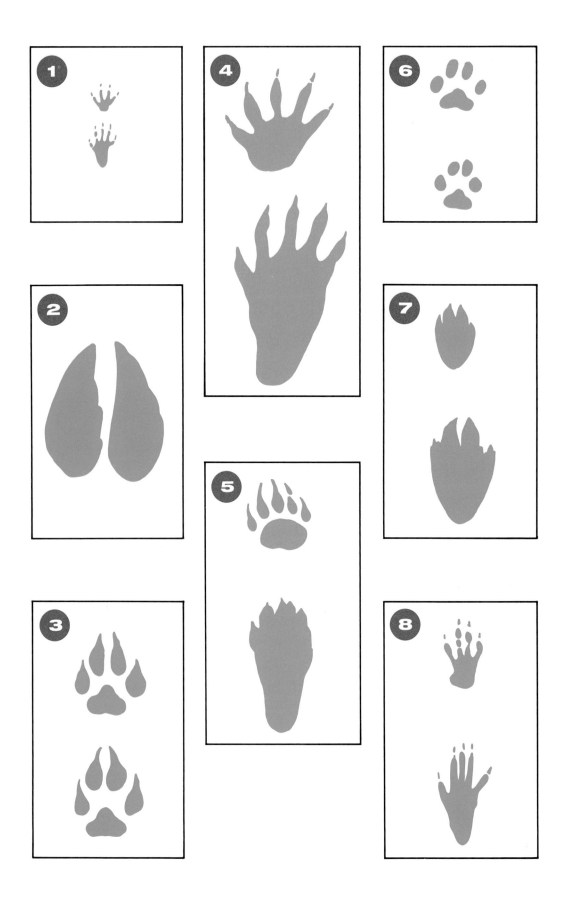

Animal Tracks

Have you ever made a footprint in the snow or sand? Dinosaurs left large footprints in the earth. Footprints made by animals are called **tracks**.

On page 184 there are some animal tracks you might find in a park or in a forest. At the bottom of this page, you can learn which animals made these tracks.

If you go looking for animal tracks, study the ground carefully. Now you might be able to recognize animal tracks when you see them.

1 MOUSE

2 DEER

3 DOG

4 RACCOON

5 SKUNK

6 CAT

7 RABBIT

8 SQUIRREL

Martin Luther King, Jr.

by David A. Adler

illustrated by Robert Casilla

Martin Luther King, Jr. was one of America's great leaders. He was a powerful speaker, and he spoke out against laws which kept black people out of many schools and jobs. He led protests and marches demanding fair laws for all people.

Martin Luther King, Jr. was born on January 15, 1929 in Atlanta, Georgia. Martin's father was a pastor. His mother had been a teacher. Martin had an older sister, Willie Christine, and a younger brother, Alfred Daniel.

Martin (center) with his brother Alfred Daniel (left) and his sister Willie Christine (right)

Young Martin liked to play baseball, football and basketball. He liked to ride his bicycle and to sing. He often sang in his father's church.

Young Martin played in his backyard with his friends. One day he was told that two of his friends would no longer play with him, because they were white and he was black.

Martin cried. He didn't understand why the color of his skin should matter to anyone.

Martin's mother told him that many years ago black people were brought in chains to America and sold as slaves. She told him that long before Martin was born the slaves had been set free. However, there were still some people who did not treat black people fairly.

In Atlanta, where Martin lived, and elsewhere in the United States, there were "White Only" signs. Black people were not allowed in some parks, pools, hotels, restaurants and even schools. Blacks were kept out of many jobs.

Martin learned to read at home
before he was old enough to start school.
All through his childhood, he read books
about black leaders.

George Washington Carver

Harriet Tubman

Frederick Douglass

Martin was a good student. He
finished high school two years early and
was just fifteen when he entered
Morehouse College in Atlanta. At college
Martin decided to become a minister.

After Martin was graduated from Morehouse, he studied for a doctorate at Boston University. While he was there he met Coretta Scott. She was studying music. They fell in love and married.

In 1954 Martin Luther King, Jr. began his first job as a pastor in Montgomery, Alabama. The next year Rosa Parks, a black woman, was arrested in Montgomery for sitting in the "White Only" section of a bus.

Dr. Martin Luther King, Jr. led a
protest. Blacks throughout the city
refused to ride the buses. Dr. King
said, "There comes a time when people
get tired . . . of being kicked about. . . ."

One night, while Dr. King was at a meeting, someone threw a bomb onto his porch.

Martin's followers were angry. They wanted to fight. Martin told them to go home peacefully. "We must love our white brothers," he said. "We must meet hate with love."

The bus protest lasted almost a year.
When it ended there were no more
"White Only" sections on buses.

Dr. King decided to move back to Atlanta in 1960. There, he continued to lead peaceful protests against "White Only" waiting rooms, lunch counters and rest rooms. He led many marches for freedom.

202

In 1963 Dr. King led the biggest march of all — the March on Washington. More than two hundred thousand black and white people followed him. "I have a dream," he said in his speech. "I have a dream that my four little children will one day live in a nation where they will not be judged by the color of their skin but by the content of their character."

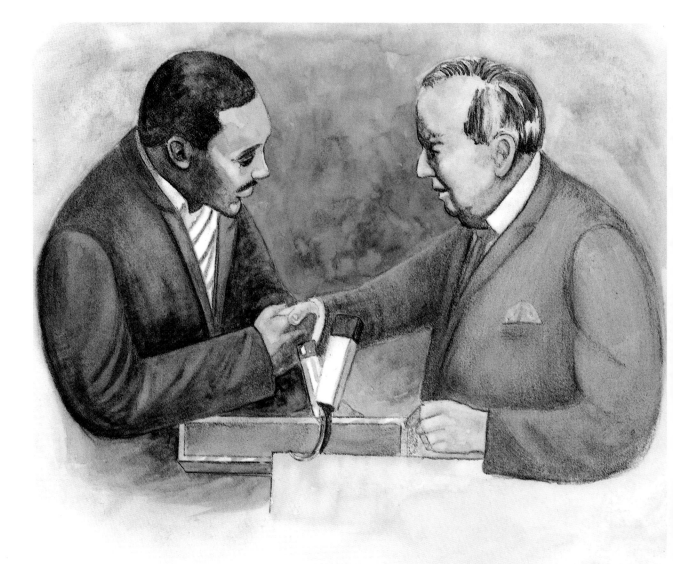

The next year in 1964, Dr. King was
awarded one of the greatest honors any
man can win, the Nobel Peace Prize.

The country was changing. New
laws were passed. Blacks could go to the
same schools as whites. They could go to
the same stores, restaurants and hotels.
"White Only" signs were against the law.

Dr. King told his followers to protest peacefully. But there were some riots and some violence.

Then, in March 1968, Dr. King went to Memphis, Tennessee. He planned to march in support of garbage workers, most of whom were black, who were striking for higher pay and better working conditions.

On April 4 in Memphis, Dr. King stood outside his motel room. Another man, James Earl Ray, was hiding nearby. He pointed a rifle at Dr. King. He fired the gun. An hour later Dr. King was dead.

Martin Luther King, Jr. dreamed of a world free of hate, prejudice and violence. Carved on the stone which marks his grave are the words, "I'm free at last."

We Have A Dream

At the March on Washington, Dr. King
made a famous speech in which he told of
his hopes and dreams for a better world.
With a partner, write a speech that tells of
your hopes and dreams for the future.
Then one of you can give your speech to
the class or both of you can take turns
reading parts of it.

About the Author

David A. Adler

David A. Adler writes nonfiction books on many different subjects — mathematics, riddles, puzzles, games, and Jewish culture. He has written biographies about George Washington, Abraham Lincoln, Helen Keller, and Thomas Edison. Some of his most popular fiction books are mysteries, including those about Cam Jansen and those about the Fourth Floor Twins.

About the Illustrator

Robert Casilla

Robert Casilla enjoys the challenge of starting a new book. Before he begins, he learns as much information as possible about the people he illustrates. He has illustrated four other books by David A. Adler, including picture books about John F. Kennedy and Eleanor Roosevelt. Robert Casilla has also illustrated *The Train to Lulu's* and *Con Mi Hermano — With My Brother.*

THE WORLD OF BOOKS

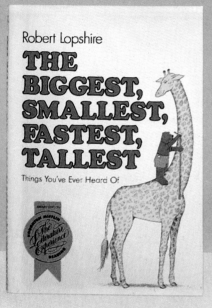

Fiesta!
by June Behrens

The fifth of May is a special holiday for Mexicans and Mexican Americans. This book shows how they celebrate it.

The Biggest, Smallest, Fastest, Tallest Things You've Ever Heard Of
by Robert Lopshire

What is the smallest horse in the world? What town has the longest name? The answers to these questions and many more are in this amazing nonfiction book.

214

A Picture Book of George Washington
by David A. Adler

Find out about the farmer who became the first president of the United States.

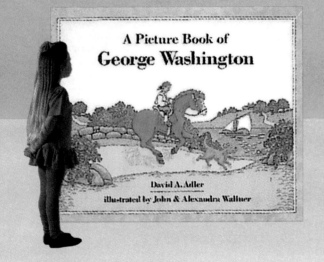

How a Book Is Made
by Aliki

This book by Aliki takes you through all the steps of how a book is made.

Rehema's Journey
by Barbara A. Margolies

This book tells about a nine-year-old girl's first trip away from home. Share the exciting sights of Tanzania, Africa, with Rehema.

Neighbors and

Thinking It Over

How are neighborhoods the same? How are they different?

Key Words

neighborhood
neighbors

R ay and Marie have just moved into a new house. They are taking a walk with their parents to explore their new **neighborhood.** They have been to the library. Now they are meeting a few of their **neighbors.**

Neighbors live near each other. They all live in the same neighborhood. The places near your home where people live, shop, work, play, and go to school are all part of your neighborhood. There are many different kinds of neighborhoods. In this lesson you will learn about three neighborhoods that are alike in some ways and different in other ways.

Neighborhoods

Thinking About Maps

Here is a map of the new neighborhood that Ray and Marie live in. The map key tells you about some of the buildings and special places on the map.

FIRE HOUSE

RAY & MARIE'S HOUSE

STORE

POLICE STATION

POOL

SCHOOL

CITY HALL

Find the school that Ray and Marie attend. What other building is nearby? Find the place where the children could go for a swim. What building is next to the police station? What other special places are shown on the map?

Joe's Neighborhood

Where Joe Lives

Houston is the biggest city in the state of Texas. Joe and his family live there, on the second floor of an apartment building. They have many neighbors in their building.

Where Joe Goes to School

Joe goes to Travis Elementary School. He walks to school with some of his neighbors. The school is only three blocks from his apartment building. It has a playground with a high fence around it. The fence keeps balls from rolling out into traffic. It keeps children from running out into the street, too.

218

Where Joe Plays

At school Joe plays in the school playground. After school he often plays baseball in the city park. He and his parents take the bus to the game. The coach is one of Joe's neighbors.

Where Joe's Family Shops for Food

Joe's grandmother goes food shopping almost every day. Sometimes Joe goes with her. They walk to the neighborhood stores and take the food home in their own shopping cart.

Stop and Think

1. What places do you see in the pictures?
2. How are these places important to Joe?

Troy's Neighborhood

Where Troy Lives

Just outside of Houston is Bay Town, where Troy lives. His house is on River Street. It has a back yard with swings for Troy and his younger brother. Sometimes Jason, Troy's next-door neighbor, comes over to play.

Where Troy Goes to School

Troy goes to Friendswood School. He takes the bus to school. The school bus stop is in front of Jason's house. On school-day mornings, Troy and the other children on River Street who go to Friendswood School wait there to be picked up. When school is over, the bus takes them back to the bus stop.

BUS STOP

Where Troy Plays

Troy and Jason are on the same soccer team. Their mothers take turns driving them to the playing field in the park for practice and for the soccer matches. The field has seats for families and friends who watch the game.

Where Troy's Family Shops for Food

Once a week Troy goes food shopping with his mother. They drive to a supermarket at an outdoor mall. They leave the car in the big parking lot. Troy finds a cart and helps his mother get the things on her list. Sometimes they fill two shopping carts!

Stop and Think

1. How is Troy's neighborhood different from Joe's neighborhood? How are they the same?

2. Why do you think Troy's family goes food shopping once a week instead of every day?

Erin's Neighborhood

Where Erin Lives

Erin lives in Belleville, a short distance from Bay Town. She lives on a ranch. Her house is set far back from the road.

Where Erin Goes to School

Erin goes to Cyprus Creek School. The school bus stops in front of her house to pick her up. In Erin's neighborhood the houses are very far apart, so the school bus stops at each student's house instead of at a bus stop. It takes a long time for Erin to get to school.

Where Erin Plays

After school Erin likes to ride her bike over to visit Sue, her next-door neighbor. Sue is raising a lamb and sometimes she lets Erin feed it. Then they shoot baskets with Sue's brother or play horseshoes.

Where Erin's Family Shops for Food

Erin goes shopping with her mom and dad on Saturday mornings. They often buy fresh vegetables at their neighbor's stand. They buy the rest of their food at a supermarket.

Review

1. Tell how Joe, Troy, and Erin each get to school. What is the same? What is different?

2. Where does each of the children play?

3. Which neighborhood is like your neighborhood? Tell how.

4. What is one way neighborhoods are the same? What is one way they are different?

Glossary

This glossary can help you find out the meanings of some of the words in this book. The meanings given are the meanings of the words as the words are used in the book. Sometimes a second meaning is also given.

adventure An event that is new and exciting: *It was an adventure when I flew in a plane for the first time.*

allowed To let someone do something: *We were not allowed to go outside after dark.*

amazing Surprising: *That is an amazing ending to the story.*

arrested Taken and held by the police for breaking a law: *Rosa Parks was arrested for sitting in the front of a bus.*

beak The hard, pointed mouth, or bill, of a bird: *The duckbill dinosaur had a wide, flat beak.*

beak

bother To worry or trouble: *My little brother always comes to bother me when I am doing my homework.*

brag To talk about yourself or things you have done: *Mark kept bragging to everyone that he got an "A" on the test.*

C
---

character What a person is like. A person's character causes him or her to think, act, or feel a certain way: *Martin Luther King's character caused him to ask for fair treatment for all people.*

claw A sharp nail on the toe of an animal or bird: *Some birds use their claws to hold on to tree branches.*

claw

club A long, heavy stick used as a weapon: *Some dinosaurs had tails shaped like clubs and used them to fight off other dinosaurs.*

club

collection A group of things that a person gathers and keeps together as a hobby: *Nan has stamps from all over the world in her stamp collection.*

craving A strong wish or longing: *Lila has a craving for chicken.*

D
---

delicious Tasting or smelling very good: *The pizza was delicious.*

deliver To bring or carry: *The flower shop will* **deliver** *the flowers to our house.*

difficult Hard: *Learning to skate was* **difficult** *for me because I fell down a lot.*

draw **1.** To make a picture with a pencil or crayons: *Jeanne likes to* **draw** *pictures of trees.* **2.** To pull together to close. To draw the curtains means to close them.

dull Not having a sharp edge or point: *The pencil was so* **dull** *that it was hard to write with it.*

dust **1.** To remove dirt by wiping or brushing: **Dust** *the shelves before you put the books back on them.* **2.** To sprinkle as if with dust: **Dust** *the chicken with flour before you put it in the pan.*

E

enemy One who hurts or wants to hurt another: *The cat is an* **enemy** *of the mouse.*

erase To remove by rubbing or wiping: *He wrote the wrong answer, so he* **erased** *it.*

exclaim To speak suddenly and loudly, as if surprised: *"Look what I found!" Jill* **exclaimed.**

F

fasten To attach one thing to another: *Carol used tape to* **fasten** *the string to the kite.*

fire To let go or send away from a job: *Bob was* **fired** *from his job because he didn't work very hard.*

flare A sudden burst of light. Stars shoot off huge red flares.

flare

I

improve To get better: *My grades improved after I began studying harder.*

J

jaws The pair of bones in the mouth that hold the teeth.

jaws

jerk To move suddenly and sharply: *When my dog pulled on his leash, the leash jerked in my hand.*

journey A long trip: *They made the long journey by ship.*

K

kite A light wooden frame covered with cloth, paper, or plastic: *We are going to fly our kite on the next windy day.*

L

language Spoken or written speech. People use language to tell one another what they think or how they feel.

law A rule that people follow when living together in a large group: *The laws were changed so that people could live wherever they wanted.*

lonely Sad at being alone: *When no one can play with me, I feel lonely.*

march The act of a group of people walking together to show that they want a change: *The **marches** in the 1960's showed that some people did not like the way they were treated.*

march

master Someone who is very good at something: *She is a **master** at drawing people.*

masterpiece A work of art done by someone who is a very good artist: *That painting is a **masterpiece**.*

measure To find the size or amount of something: *Dad will **measure** the floor to be sure to buy a rug that is the right size.*

meringue A topping for pies, made of beaten egg whites: *Meg baked a lemon **meringue** pie.*

million A very large number. A million is a larger number than a thousand: *There are **millions** of stars in the sky.*

modestly In a way that shows that someone does not want to brag about his or her own work or talent: *When his pie won first prize, Jeff **modestly** said it was not that good.*

mope To be sad and silent: *When it rained and she couldn't go camping, Beth **moped** around the house.*

P

peacefully In a calm and quiet way: *The two players were angry with each other, but after the game they **peacefully** shook hands.*

perfect Very good in every way: *A sunny day is* ***perfect*** *for going to the beach.*

perform To sing, dance, or do something else in front of a group of people: *All the people in our neighborhood came to see us* ***perform*** *our play.*

portrait A picture of a person or animal. Often the picture is only of the face: *A* ***portrait*** *of my grandmother is on the table in the den.*

portrait

practice Something done over and over in order to become good at it: *It takes a lot of* ***practice*** *to play the piano well.*

prejudice A strong feeling or idea that is often unfair to one person or group of people. People with a prejudice have their minds made up before they know all the facts.

prey An animal hunted by another animal for food: *Chickens are the* ***prey*** *of wolves.*

promise To say that you will do something: *I* ***promised*** *my mother that I would clean my room today.*

protest An action that shows that someone does not agree with an idea or action: *The neighbors kept up their* ***protests*** *until the store agreed to lower its prices.*

refuse To be unwilling to do something: *He* **refused** *to walk home in the dark.*

reunion A time when people who have been apart get back together again: *After three months at camp I had a* **reunion** *with my parents.*

riot The behavior of a large group of people who are angry and noisy: *The* **riots** *started when a few people in the crowd began pushing.*

rocket A powerful aircraft that burns fuel very fast.

rocket

scrumptious Very tasty and delicious: *The baker made* **scrumptious** *cookies and cakes that everyone loved.*

seriously In a way that is not fooling or joking: *Pete wondered what was wrong when his father spoke so* **seriously**.

sharp Pointed or having a thin edge that cuts: *The knife is not* **sharp** *enough to cut the meat.*

sigh To let out a long, deep breathing sound because one is sad or tired: *Juan* **sighed** *unhappily when I told him I was moving away.*

snip To cut with short, quick movements: *Sally* **snipped** *the cloth with her scissors.*

snip

snort To make a loud sound by forcing air through the nose: *The horse* **snorted** *loudly when we came near it.*

space The area in which the sun, stars, and planets are found.

stew A thick soup that is cooked very slowly. A chicken stew might be made of chicken, vegetables, and water.

stew

still 1. Now as before: *Ann* **still** *doesn't know how to whistle.* **2.** Not moving: *Sit* **still** *while I take your picture.*

swirl To spin or move in circles very quickly: *The snowflakes* **swirled** *around in the strong wind.*

swoop To fly or move in a sudden sweeping way: *A large bird* **swooped** *down from the sky.*

tail 1. The string or cloth that hangs from the bottom of a kite to help the kite fly straight: *Gloria carefully tied pieces of rags to the kite's* **tail**. **2.** The part of an animal's body that is farthest to the rear: *When dogs are happy, they wag their* **tails**.

tease To bother someone by making fun of him or her: *My uncle used to **tease** me about being taller than all my cousins.*

terrible Very bad: *The movie was so **terrible** that we all left before it was over.*

terrific Very good: *It was a **terrific** party.*

thousand A large number. A thousand is a larger number than a hundred.

travel To go from one place to another: *We **traveled** by car to my grandparents' house.*

trim **1.** To make neat or even by cutting. To trim the fat from the meat means to cut the fat away. **2.** To make fancy or beautiful: *Lisa **trimmed** the box with ribbons and bows.*

twinkle To shine with quick flashes of light: *Stars **twinkle** in the sky at night.*

unscrew To remove by twisting: *My mother **unscrewed** the old light bulb and put in a new one.*

unusual Not happening often or all the time: *It is **unusual** for John to walk to school because most days his father drives him.*

violence The use of force to hurt someone or something: *My aunt does not like all the **violence** on TV.*

Acknowledgments

For each of the selections listed below, grateful acknowledgment is made for permission to excerpt and/or reprint original or copyrighted material, as follows:

Major Selections

Amelia Bedelia, by Peggy Parish, illustrated by Fritz Siebel. Text copyright © 1963 by Margaret Parish. Illustrations copyright © 1963 by Fritz Siebel. Reprinted by permission of Harper & Row, Publishers, Inc.

Dinosaur Time, by Peggy Parish. Text copyright © 1974 by Margaret Parish. Illustrations copyright © 1974 by Arnold Lobel. Reprinted by permission of Harper & Row, Publishers, Inc.

Do You Know About Stars? by Mae Blacker Freeman. Copyright © 1970 by Mae Blacker Freeman. Reprinted by permission of Random House, Inc.

"Gloria Who Might Be My Best Friend," from *The Stories Julian Tells*, by Ann Cameron. Copyright © 1981 by Ann Cameron. Reprinted by permission of Pantheon Books, a division of Random House, Inc., and Victor Gollancz Ltd.

Ira Says Goodbye, by Bernard Waber. Copyright © 1988 by Bernard Waber. Reprinted by permission of Houghton Mifflin Company and Curtis Brown, Ltd.

"Martin Luther King, Jr.," published as *A Picture Book of Martin Luther King, Jr.* by David A. Adler, illustrated by Robert Casilla. Text copyright © 1989 by David A. Adler. Illustrations copyright © 1989 by Robert Casilla. All rights reserved. Reprinted by permission of Holiday House, Inc.

"My First American Friend" by Sarunna Jin. Copyright © 1991, Raintree Publishers Limited Partnership. Reprinted with permission.

The Portrait (Garabato) by Ivar Da Coll. Copyright © Ivar Da Coll. Translated and reprinted by permission of Carlos Valencia Editores, S.A.

The Wolf's Chicken Stew, by Keiko Kasza. Copyright © 1987 by Keiko Kasza. Reprinted by permission of G. P. Putnam's Sons and Geoffrey Bles, Ltd.

Poetry

"At the Beach," by John Ciardi, from *Doodle Soup*. Copyright © 1985 by Myra J. Ciardi. Reprinted by permission of Houghton Mifflin Company.

"Banananananananana," by William Cole. Copyright © 1977 by William Cole. Reprinted by permission of the author.

"Cow in the City" from *The Butterfly Jar* by Jeff Moss. Copyright © 1989 by Jeff Moss. Reprinted by permission of Bantam Books, a division of Bantam Doubleday Dell Publishing Group, and International Creative Management Ltd.

"Eletelephony," by Laura E. Richards, from *Tirra Lirra: Rhymes Old and New*. Copyright 1930, 1932 by Laura E. Richards. Copyright © renewed 1960 by Hamilton Richards. Reprinted by permission of Little, Brown and Company.

"The Folk Who Live in Backward Town," in *Hello and Good-By*, by Mary Ann Hoberman. Copyright © 1959 by Mary Ann Hoberman, renewed 1987. Reprinted by permission of the Gina Maccoby Literary Agency.

"If I Find a Penny" from *The Butterfly Jar* by Jeff Moss. Copyright © 1989 by Jeff Moss. Reprinted by permission of Bantam Books, a division of Bantam Doubleday Dell Publishing Group, and International Creative Management Ltd.

"In Between" from *The Butterfly Jar* by Jeff Moss. Copyright © 1989 by Jeff Moss. Reprinted by permission of Bantam Books, a division of Bantam Doubleday Dell Publishing Group, and International Creative Management Ltd.

"Moving" from *The Butterfly Jar* by Jeff Moss. Copyright © 1989 by Jeff Moss. Reprinted by permission of Bantam Books, a division of Bantam Doubleday Dell Publishing Group, and International Creative Management Ltd.

"My Fat Cat" from *The Tamarindo Puppy and Other Poems* by Charlotte Pomerantz, illustrated by Byron Barton. Copyright © 1980 by Charlotte Pomerantz. Reprinted by permission of William Morrow and Company, Inc., Publishers, New York.

"Once in the Streets of Caracas" ("Una vez, por las calles de Caracas") from *Zoo Loco* by Maria Elena Walsh. Copyright © 1980, Editorial Sudamericana. Reprinted by permission of Editorial Sudamericana.

"A puppy whose hair was so flowing," by Oliver Herford. Copyright 1912 The Century Co.

"Since Hanna Moved Away," by Judith Viorst, from *If I Were in Charge of the World and Other Worries*. Copyright © 1981 by Judith Viorst. Reprinted by permission of Atheneum Publishers, an imprint of Macmillan Publishing Company, and Lescher and Lescher.

"There was a sad pig with a tail," by Arnold Lobel. Copyright © 1983 by Arnold Lobel. Reprinted from *The Book of Pigericks* by permission of Harper & Row, Publishers, Inc.

"Two Friends," by Nikki Giovanni, from *Spin a Soft Black Song*. Copyright © 1971 by Nikki Giovanni. Reprinted by permission of Farrar, Straus and Giroux.

"What Johnny Told Me," by John Ciardi, from *Fast and Slow*. Copyright 1975 by John Ciardi. Reprinted by permission of Houghton Mifflin Company.

Credits

Program Design   Carbone Smolan Associates

Cover Design   Carbone Smolan Associates

Design   8–11, 26–67, 72–73 TextArt;   12–25, 68–71 Joy Chu Design;   74–77 Ann Potter;   78–137 DeFrancis Studio; 138–215 Sheaff Design, Inc.;   216–223 Carbone Smolan Associates

Introduction   (left to right) 1st row: Fred Schrier; Frank Siteman; Fred Schrier;   2nd row: J. Running; Cat Bowman Smith; Fred Lynch;   3rd row: Tom Garcia; Fred Schrier; Cat Bowman Smith;   4th row: Fred Schrier; Gerald & Buff Corsi/Tom Stack & Associates; James L. Ballard

Table of Contents   5 Cat Bowman Smith;   6 Fred Schrier; 7 Sheaff Design, Inc.

Illustration   8–11 Cat Bowman Smith;   12 (calligraphy) Joyce Y. L. Chu;   12–25 Jean and Mou-sien Tseng;   26–27 Cat Bowman Smith;   28–52 Bernard Waber;   53 Cat Bowman Smith;   54–66 Beth Peck;   67–73 Cat Bowman Smith;   75–77 Catharine O'Neill;   78–81 Fred Schrier; 82–92 Keiko Kasza;   93 Fred Schrier;   94–110 Ivar Da Coll;   111 Fred Schrier;   112–119 T. R. Garcia;   120–132 Fritz Siebel;   133–137 Fred Schrier;   138–141 Bob Brangwynne;   142–157 Fred Lynch;   162–181 Arnold Lobel;   186–211 Robert Casilla;   214–215 Bob Brangwynne;   216–223 Leslie Wolf;   224, 225, 227 (top), 231 (bottom)   Meg Kelleher-Aubrey;   227 (bottom), 228, 229, 231 (top) Jan Palmer

Photography   12 Courtesy of Jingmin Jin;   68 Courtesy of Jingmin Jin;   69 Courtesy of Jean and Mou-sien Tseng;   70 Courtesy of Bernard Waber (bottom right);   71 Das Anudas; 71 Courtesy of Beth Peck (bottom);   74 Courtesy of Jeff Moss;   134 Courtesy of G. P. Putnam's Sons;   134 Sergio Barbosa/Courtesy of Ivar Da Coll (bottom);   135 Courtesy of Gretchen Siebel, Siebel Mohr Inc. (bottom);   135 Rick Foster/Reprinted courtesy of HarperCollins Children's Books (top);   159 Courtesy of Something About the Author;   159 Courtesy of Fred Lynch (bottom left);   160 Gerald & Buff Corsi/Tom Stack and Associates;   183 Reprinted courtesy of HarperCollins Children's Books;   183 Van Williams (bottom); 212 F. Miller © Time, Inc. 1963 (bottom);   213 David A. Adler (top); Courtesy of Robert Casilla (bottom);   225 Royce Blair/Stock Solution;   230 Grant Heilman Photography; **Assignment Photographers**   Richard Haynes 161, 185. Sam Gray 138–139, 141, 214–215. Janice Rubin 218–223.